AF598969

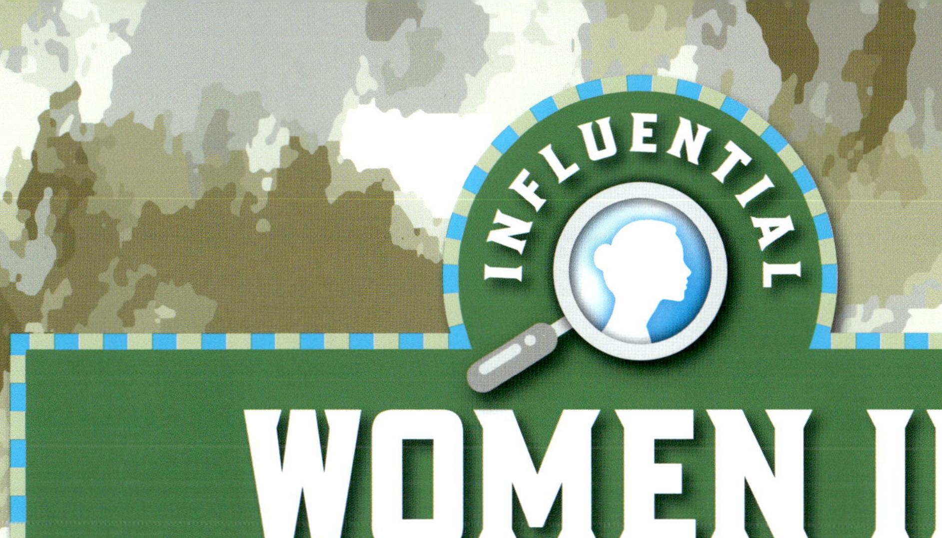

INFLUENTIAL

WOMEN IN THE MILITARY

EMMA KAISER

childsworld.com

Published by The Child's World®
800-599-READ • www.childsworld.com

Photography Credits
Photographs ©: Staff Sgt. Carmen Fleischmann/DVIDS, cover (soldier), 1 (soldier); MSK Design/Shutterstock Images, cover (background), 1 (background), 3 (background); Alexander Skowalsky/Noun Project, cover (icon), 1 (icon), 3 (icon), back cover; Sgt. Sinthia Rosario/DVIDS, 5, 22; John Eric Jackson/Shutterstock Images, 6; Philip Cuddy/US Department of Defense, 9; Stan Rohrer/Alamy, 10–11; Eboni Everson-Myart/DVIDS, 13; Sgt. Matthew Lucibello/US Army/DVIDS, 16–17; Patrick Albright/US Army/DVIDS, 18–19; Staff Sgt. Steve Cortez/US Army/DVIDS, 20

ISBN Information
9781503889576 (Reinforced Library Binding)
9781503890305 (Portable Document Format)
9781503891548 (Online Multi-user eBook)
9781503892781 (Electronic Publication)

LCCN 2023950451

Printed in the United States of America

Emma Kaiser is a writer and educator based in western Minnesota. She has a master of fine arts (MFA) in creative writing from the University of Minnesota, and her writing has appeared in a number of magazines and publications. She is the author of several other nonfiction books for students.

TABLE OF CONTENTS

CATHAY WILLIAMS

In 1844, Cathay Williams was born into slavery in Independence, Missouri. She remained enslaved until after the US Civil War (1861–1865). This war was fought between Northern Union states and Southern Confederate states over the South's right to practice slavery. In 1861, the Union Army came to the city Williams lived in. She was forced to follow the army and work as a cook. She decided she wanted to join the army as a soldier instead.

Soldier Nettie J. Thomas (center) received an award while dressed as Cathay Williams.

Williams signed up in 1866. At that time, the army did not allow women to serve. To join, she had to disguise herself as a man. She went by the name William Cathay. She became the first Black woman to **enlist** in the US Army.

The Buffalo Soldiers are honored by this monument at Fort Leavenworth, Kansas.

WOMEN IN DISGUISE

There were other women who posed as men to join the military. Sarah Emma Edmonds enlisted in the Union Army during the US Civil War. She went by the name Franklin Flint Thompson. After the war, she wrote about her experience as a soldier.

Williams served in the army for two years. Then she became sick with smallpox in 1868. Doctors came to treat her. They discovered she was a woman. She was **honorably discharged**.

Williams did not give up. She disguised herself as a man again. She joined the 38th US **Infantry**. The 38th Infantry was made up of Black men. This group, along with others, would become known as the Buffalo Soldiers.

Williams had poor health after her time in the army. She died in 1893. It would still be many years before women were allowed to serve in the US military.

SUSAN AHN CUDDY

Susan Ahn Cuddy was born in 1915 in Los Angeles, California. Cuddy's parents had moved there from Korea in 1902. They raised Cuddy to be adventurous and independent.

Cuddy was a young woman during World War II (1939–1945). At first, the United States did not join the war. But in 1941, Japan attacked the US naval base at Pearl Harbor in Hawaii. More than 2,400 people died. The United States entered the war. Cuddy wanted to help.

Susan Ahn Cuddy (right) shows a sailor how to use a machine gun.

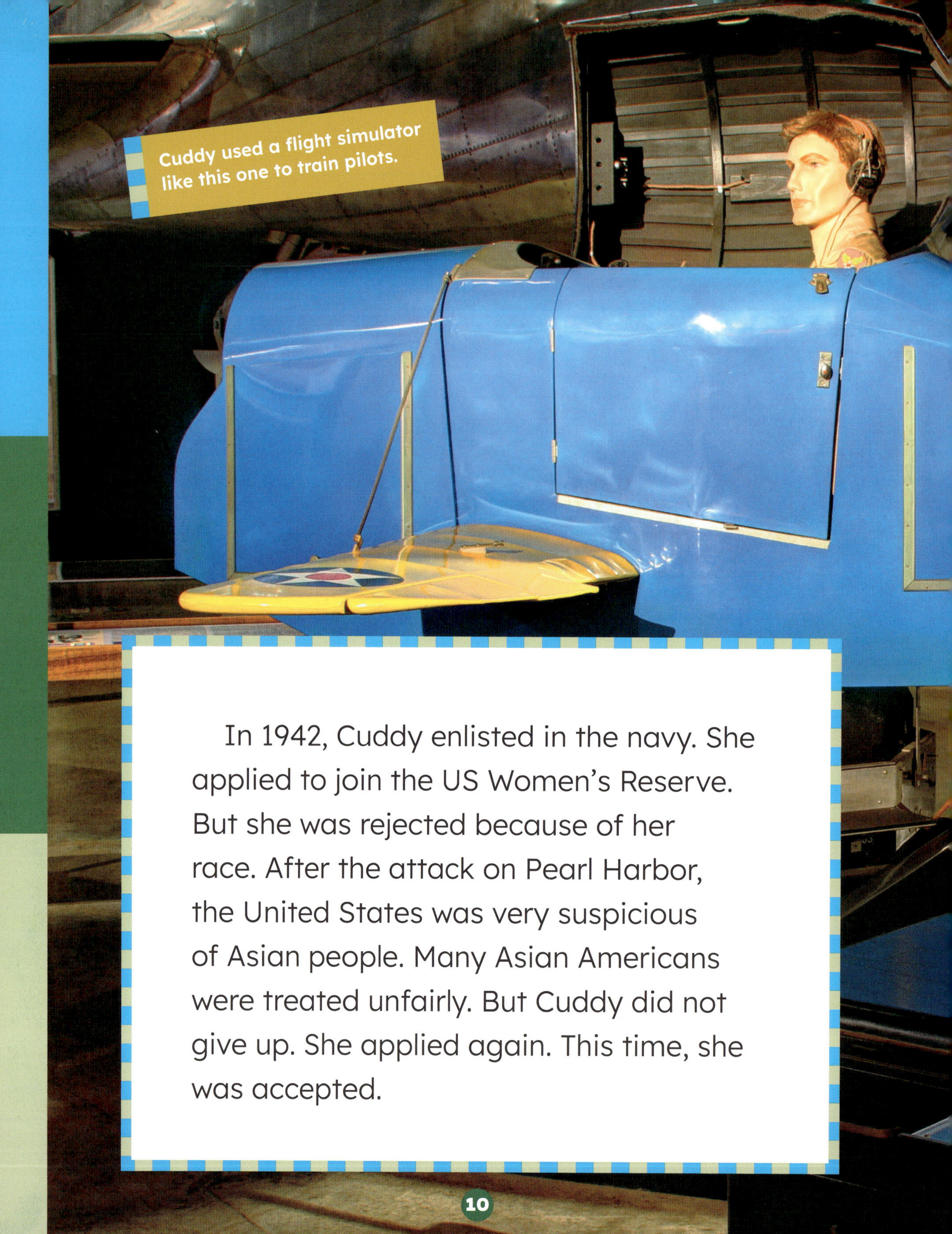

Cuddy used a flight simulator like this one to train pilots.

In 1942, Cuddy enlisted in the navy. She applied to join the US Women's Reserve. But she was rejected because of her race. After the attack on Pearl Harbor, the United States was very suspicious of Asian people. Many Asian Americans were treated unfairly. But Cuddy did not give up. She applied again. This time, she was accepted.

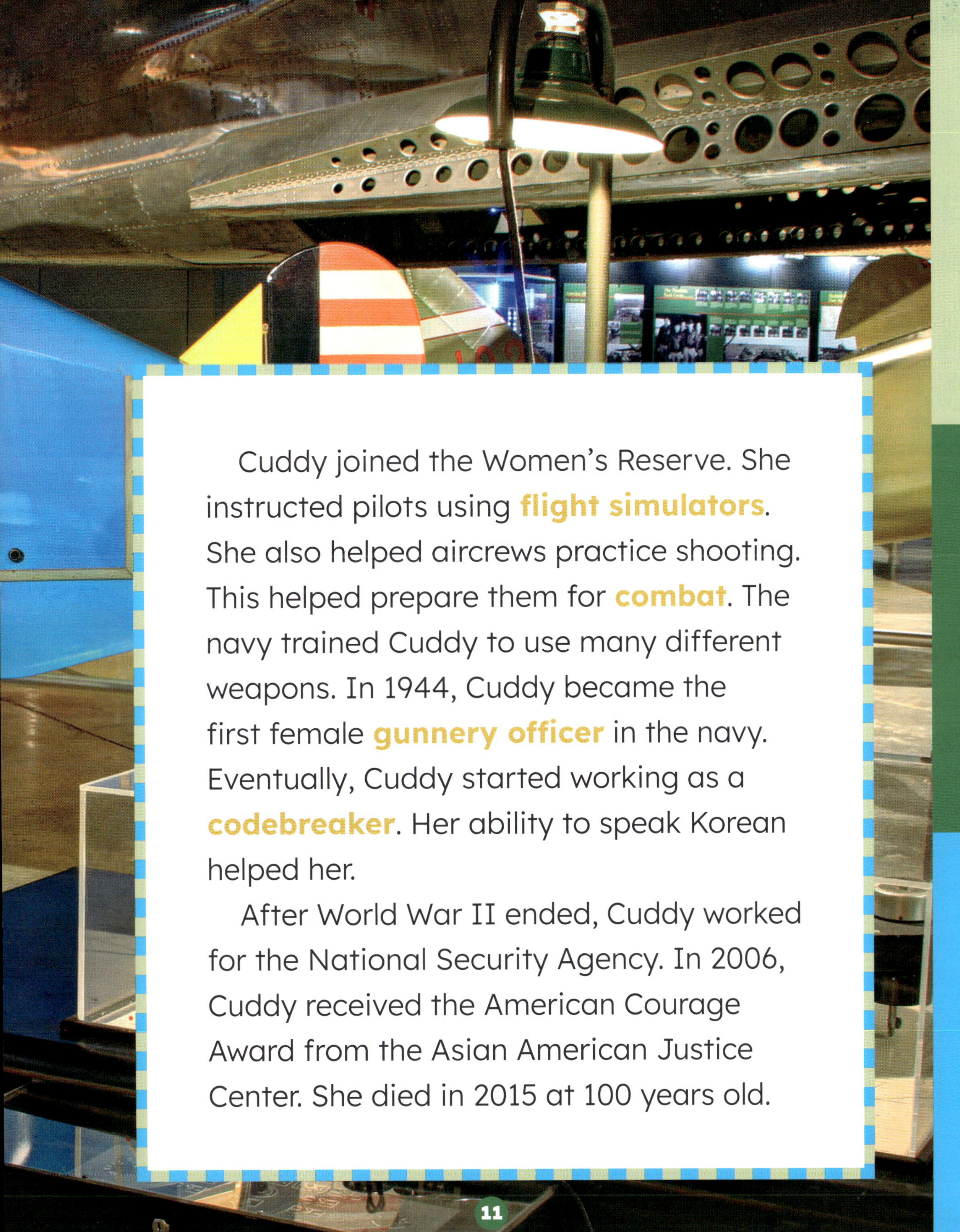

Cuddy joined the Women's Reserve. She instructed pilots using **flight simulators**. She also helped aircrews practice shooting. This helped prepare them for **combat**. The navy trained Cuddy to use many different weapons. In 1944, Cuddy became the first female **gunnery officer** in the navy. Eventually, Cuddy started working as a **codebreaker**. Her ability to speak Korean helped her.

After World War II ended, Cuddy worked for the National Security Agency. In 2006, Cuddy received the American Courage Award from the Asian American Justice Center. She died in 2015 at 100 years old.

ANN E. DUNWOODY

Ann E. Dunwoody was born in 1953 to a military family. Her father, grandfather, and great-grandfather were all **veterans**. She grew up on different military bases. But as a kid, Dunwoody wasn't particularly interested in the military. That changed when she went to college. She joined an army introductory program in 1974.

After graduating from college, Dunwoody joined the US Women's Army Corps. She became a second lieutenant. She learned how to jump out of airplanes.

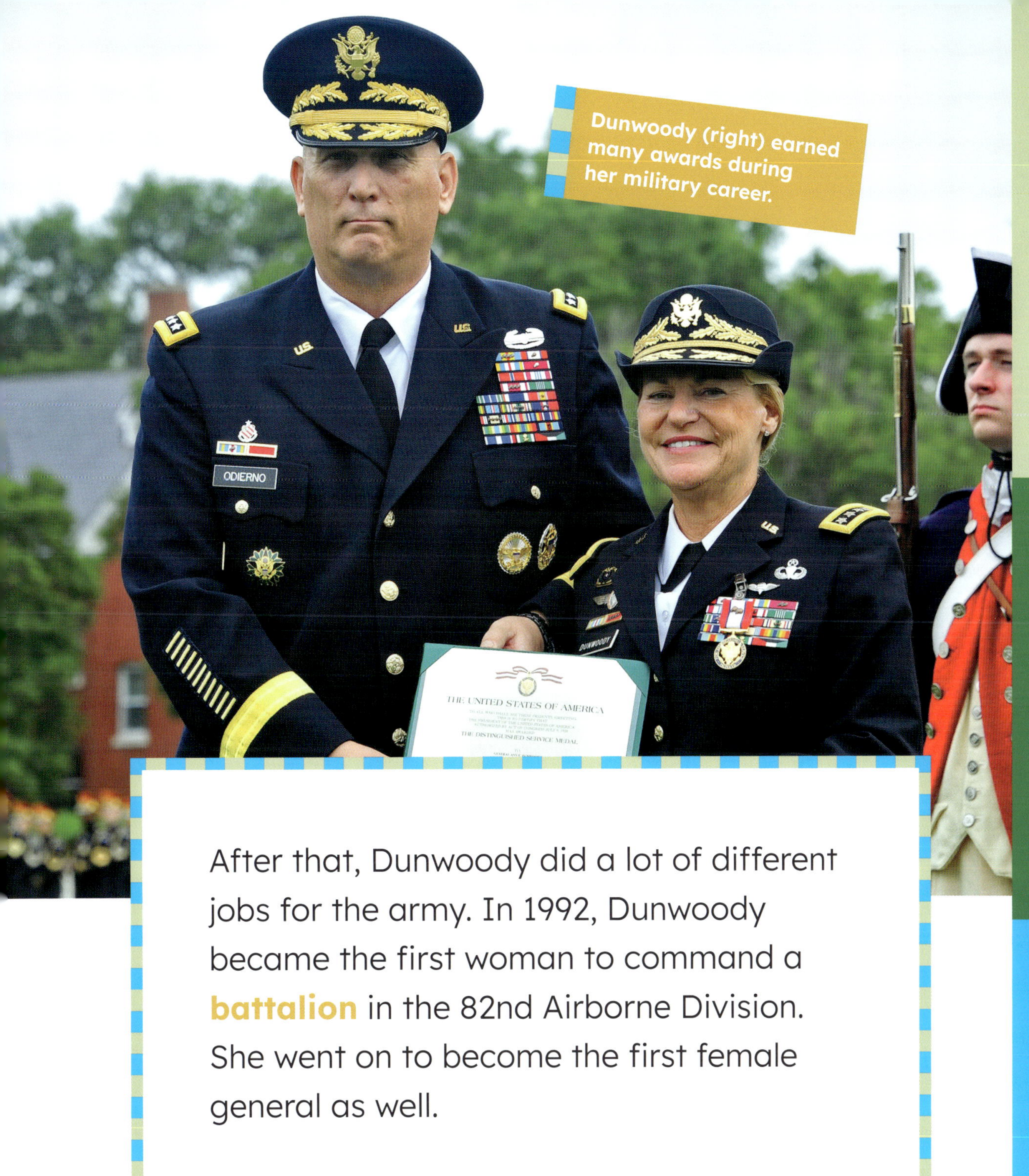

Dunwoody (right) earned many awards during her military career.

After that, Dunwoody did a lot of different jobs for the army. In 1992, Dunwoody became the first woman to command a **battalion** in the 82nd Airborne Division. She went on to become the first female general as well.

One of her most important assignments came in 2008. She served as commander of one of the largest **commands** in the army. This command is called the Army Materiel Command (AMC). Dunwoody was in charge of 69,000 people across all 50 US states and 145 countries. While at the AMC, Dunwoody became a four-star general. This is the highest rank a general can earn. She was the first woman to do so.

Dunwoody retired in 2012. She served in the military for 38 years. She says there is nothing else she would have rather done with her life.

TIMELINE OF WOMEN IN THE MILITARY

Women have fought for their place in the US military for more than 100 years.

1917
Women are allowed to openly serve in the military during World War I (1914–1918).

1942
Women are allowed to perform non-combat roles in the US Army.

1948
Women are allowed to become permanent members of the military.

2008
First woman is promoted to the rank of general.

2013
Women are allowed to serve in combat roles on land, at sea, and in the air.

2016
Women are allowed to serve in all military positions.

KRISTEN GRIEST

Kristen Griest was born in 1989 in Connecticut. As a child, she was determined to compete with the boys her age. After graduating from high school, she attended West Point Military Academy. There, she trained to meet the same standards set for the men. After graduating in 2011, Griest became a second lieutenant. She was sent to Afghanistan in 2013. She led more than 100 missions. She earned a Bronze Star Medal for her service in Afghanistan.

In 2022, Griest was promoted to the rank of major.

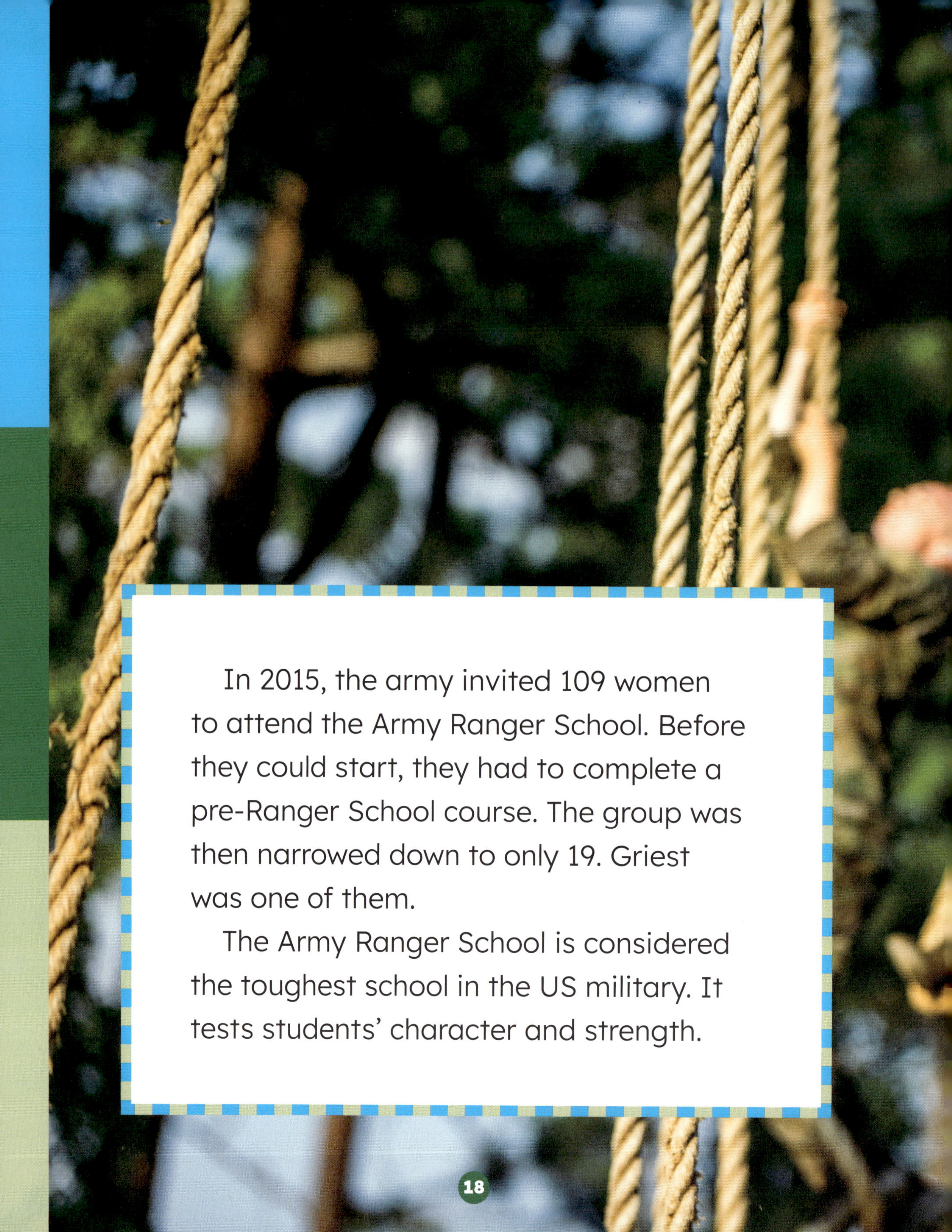

In 2015, the army invited 109 women to attend the Army Ranger School. Before they could start, they had to complete a pre-Ranger School course. The group was then narrowed down to only 19. Griest was one of them.

The Army Ranger School is considered the toughest school in the US military. It tests students' character and strength.

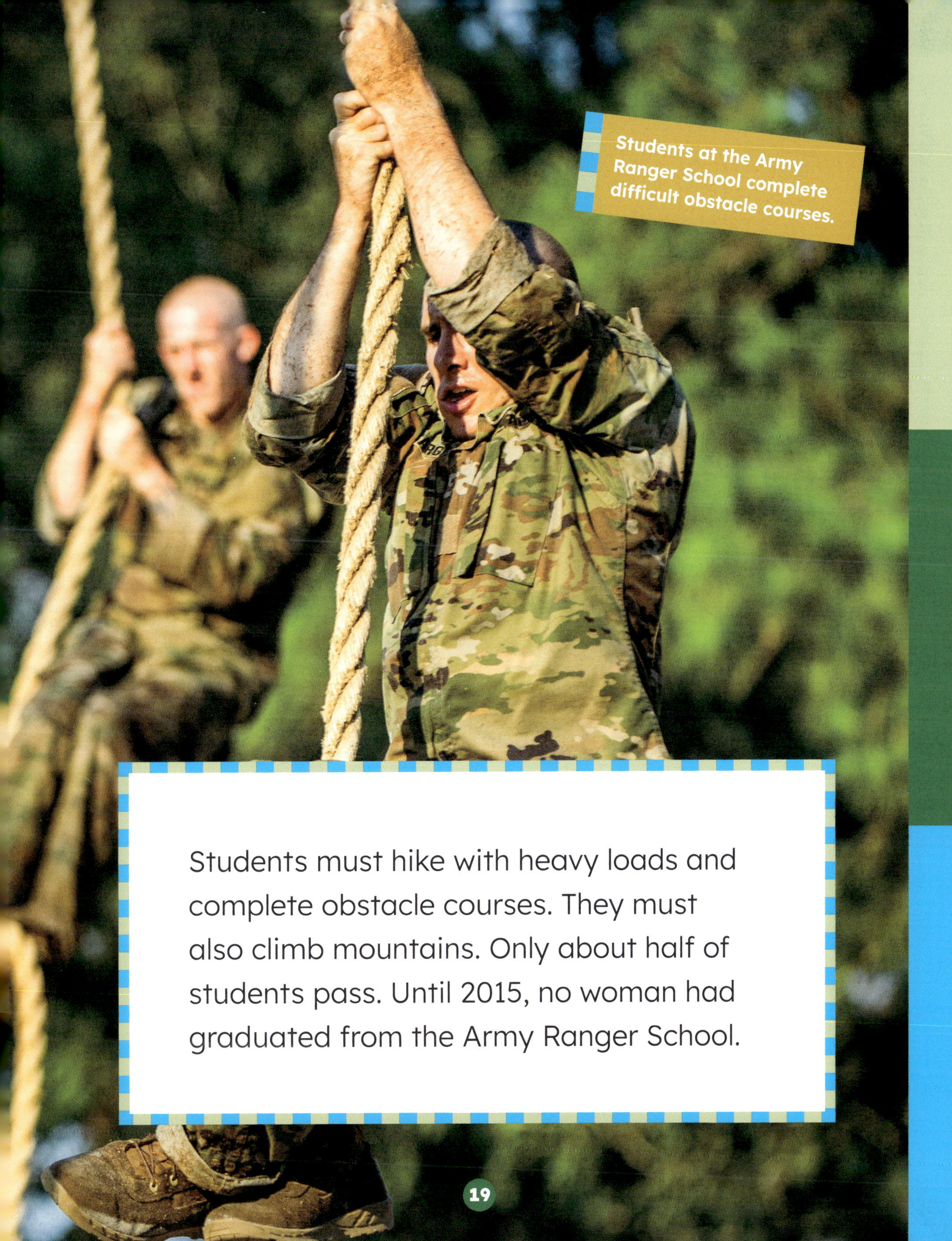

Students at the Army Ranger School complete difficult obstacle courses.

Students must hike with heavy loads and complete obstacle courses. They must also climb mountains. Only about half of students pass. Until 2015, no woman had graduated from the Army Ranger School.

Griest (right) salutes during her graduation ceremony from the Army Ranger School.

Griest's training involved many hard tests. She had to repeat some of them. But on August 21, 2015, Griest became one of the first women to complete the training school. Shaye Lynne Haver was the other woman to graduate that day. They proved to the military that women were tough enough to handle extreme physical challenges. Beginning in 2016, the US military made all positions open to women for the first time.

WONDER MORE

Wondering about New Information

How much did you know about women in the military before reading this book? What new information did you learn? Write down three new facts that this book taught you. Was the new information surprising? Why or why not?

Wondering How It Matters

What is one way the military relates to your life? If you cannot think of a personal connection, imagine a way the topic might affect other kids. What impact might it have on their lives?

Wondering Why

Women have made many contributions to the military. But they have also been excluded in many ways. Why do you think this is? Why do you think it is important for women to be included?

Ways to Keep Wondering

There is a long and complex history of women's participation in the military. After reading this book, what questions do you have about this topic? What can you do to learn more about women in the military?

FAST FACTS

- Cathay Williams was born into slavery in 1844. She changed her name to William Cathay in order to enlist in the army. She was the first Black woman to serve in the army.
- Many women disguised themselves as men in order to serve in the military.
- Susan Ahn Cuddy was born in Los Angeles, California, after her parents moved to the United States from Korea. At first, she was rejected from the US Navy because of her race. But during World War II, she became the first female naval gunnery officer.
- In 2008, Ann E. Dunwoody became the first woman to earn the rank of four-star general.
- Kristen Griest and Shaye Lynne Haver became the first women to graduate from the Army Ranger School in 2015.
- In 2016, the US military opened all positions to women.

GLOSSARY

battalion (buh-TAL-yun) A battalion is an organized group of up to 1,000 soldiers. Ann E. Dunwoody commanded a battalion.

codebreaker (KODE-bray-kur) A codebreaker is someone who figures out how to read messages written in a secret code. Susan Ahn Cuddy served as a codebreaker during World War II.

combat (KOM-bat) Combat is violent fighting between opposing forces. Soldiers can be sent into combat.

commands (kuh-MANDZ) Commands are groups of soldiers led by a commander. The AMC is one of the largest commands in the army.

enlist (en-LIST) To enlist means to join the military. Women and men can both enlist in the US Army.

flight simulators (FLITE SIM-yuh-lay-turz) Flight simulators are tools that help pilots practice flying. Susan Ahn Cuddy helped pilots use flight simulators.

gunnery officer (GUH-nur-ree AW-fiss-ur) A gunnery officer is a person in the US Navy in charge of a ship's guns. Susan Ahn Cuddy served as a gunnery officer during World War II.

honorably discharged (AH-nur-uh-blee DIS-charjd) To be honorably discharged is to be given a positive review upon leaving the military. Cathay Williams was honorably discharged from the army.

infantry (IN-fuhn-tree) An infantry is a group of soldiers fighting on foot. Cathay Williams was a member of the 38th US Infantry.

veterans (VET-ur-uhnz) Veterans are people who have served in the military. There are many female veterans.

FIND OUT MORE

In the Library

Huddleston, Emma. *Civil War Spy Stories.* Parker, CO: The Child's World, 2021.

Taylor, Susan. *Women in World War Two.* New York, NY: Children's Press, 2021.

Wallmark, Laurie. *Code Breaker, Spy Hunter: How Elizebeth Friedman Changed the Course of Two World Wars.* New York, NY: Abrams Press, 2021.

On the Web

Visit our website for links about women in the military:
childsworld.com/links

Note to Parents, Caregivers, Teachers, and Librarians: We routinely verify our web links to make sure they are safe and active sites. So encourage your readers to check them out!

INDEX